Picture the Past

TOYS

Jane Shuter

Heinemann
LIBRARY

First published in Great Britain by Heinemann Library
Halley Court, Jordan Hill, Oxford OX2 8EJ
a division of Reed Educational & Professional Publishing Ltd

OXFORD FLORENCE PRAGUE MADRID ATHENS
MELBOURNE AUCKLAND KUALA LUMPUR SINGAPORE TOKYO
IBADAN NAIROBI KAMPALA JOHANNESBURG GABORONE
PORTSMOUTH NH (USA) CHICAGO MEXICO CITY SAO PAULO

Designed by Ken Vail Graphic Design, Cambridge
Colour separations by Dot Gradations, Wickford, Essex
Printed in Malaysia by Times Offset (M) Sdn. Bhd.

01 00 99 98 97
10 9 8 7 6 5 4 3 2 1

ISBN 0 431 04270 5

British Library Cataloguing in Publication Data

Shuter, Jane
  Toys – (Picture the past)
  1. Toys – History – Juvenile literature
  2. Toys – Pictorial works – Juvenile literature
  I. Title
  688.7'2'09

Acknowledgements
The authors and publishers would like to thank the following for permission to use
photographs and other illustrative material:

Beck Isle Museum, page 4 top;
The Peter Gillies Collection, page 4 bottom;
Oxfordshire Photographic Archive, pages 5, 12;
Suffolk Photographic Survey, page 6;
Topham Picturepoint, pages 8, 10, 14, 16, 18, 20.

Cover photographs reproduced with permission of Oxfordshire Photographic
Archive and Topham Picturepoint.

Our thanks to Betty Root for her comments in the preparation of this book.

Every effort has been made to contact copyright holders of any material reproduced
in this book. Any omissions will be rectified in subsequent printings if notice is
given to the Publisher.

Contents

Some words are shown in bold text, **like this**. You can find out what these words mean by looking in the glossary on page 24.

Taking photos

People started taking photos in the 1830s. It took over an hour to take a photo! By the 1860s it only took 15 minutes.

When cameras were first invented, they could only take black and white photos. If people wanted colour photos, they had to paint them by hand.

Children have always had the same sorts of toys, like dolls and toy animals. The doll in this photo (taken in 1900) has a **china** head and a cloth body. The horse on wheels is made of wood. Now many toys are made of plastic.

Nursery toys, 1904

The mothers of these children worked in a **factory** in Ipswich. The children are playing in this nursery while their mothers work.

The buckets and spades are made of wood and metal.

The children take turns to ride the rocking horse.

The **nannies** look after the babies, while the older children play.

Can you find
- a big pram full of babies?
- a toy dog?
- four hats that are the same?

Sand-pit toys, 1910

These children are playing in a home-made sand-pit. It looks as if it is on a **building site**.

The buckets and spades are made from metal.

The children are all wearing hats to keep the sun off their heads.

The girls are all wearing **pinafores** to keep their clothes clean.

Can you find

- two different sorts of bucket?
- two pairs of lace-up boots?
- ten spades?

These girls are learning to sew and knit.
They are making dolls' clothes. There is only
one sewing machine for them all to use.

The dolls' faces are made of hard **plaster**.

Their bodies are made from material and stuffed with rags or straw.

To work the sewing machine, you had to turn this handle.

Can you find
- a tape measure?
- four dolls?
- your favourite hat?

School toys in about 1920

These children are having their photo taken with the class toys. Photos taken at the same school in different years show different children but the same toys.

The dolls have been put to bed in the cribs.

The **china** tea set has been put out ready for tea.

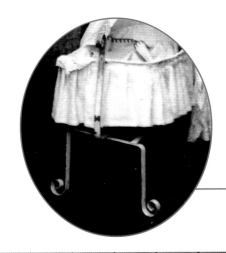

This crib has a metal stand. The stand of the other crib is made of wood.

Can you find
- the teddy?
- the play house?
- the rocking horse?

War-time toys, 1944

From 1939 to 1945 there was a war. Lots of houses in the **UK** were bombed. People in the **USA** sent toys at Christmas for children in the UK whose homes had been destroyed.

This box has pieces that can be made into a small dolls' house.

These yo-yos go up and down on long strings.

Some toys have to be made first. This box is full of pieces to glue together!

Can you find
- a box of paints?
- nine dolls?
- a box of soft toys for babies?

This little boy and his mother are
looking at the Christmas toys.
The little boy likes the teddy.

This doll is dressed as Father Christmas. How else can we tell it is Christmas?

Some people bought bare dolls and made clothes for them at home.

This set helps children dress up as a bus **conductor** who sells tickets to passengers.

Can you find
- the sailor doll?
- the target for shooting at?
- the push-along train?

School toys, 1953

This classroom is in a school which was opened in 1953. These children are the first to play with the toys in the new school.

There are books for the children to read, as well as toys for them to play with.

The tea set is made of real **china**.

The furniture in the dolls' house is just like the real furniture at the time.

What's different?

Look at the photo on page 12.

- How are things different in 1953?
- How many of the same toys can you find?

These children are looking at model railways from all over the world. They were on show at Eastbourne.

The model cars look just like real cars at the time. They are made of metal.

This is a model of a steam train. Because it is a toy, it does not use coal. Electricity makes it work.

Can you find

- a railway truck with numbers on?
- a cart for moving things around?
- eight different tracks?

Did you find?

Nursery toys, 1904,
pages 6–7

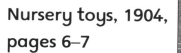

Sand-pit toys, 1910,
pages 8–9

Dolls in about 1910,
pages 10–11

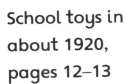

School toys in about 1920, pages 12–13

War-time toys, 1944, pages 14–15

Christmas toys, 1950, pages 16–17

Model railways, 1957, pages 20–21

Glossary (What words mean)

building site a place where builders work

china baked and painted clay. Cups and plates are often made from china

conductor someone who sells tickets on trains and buses

factory a work-place where lots of people make the same sorts of things

nannies people who look after babies and children for other people

pinafore an apron

plaster a powder which can be made into shapes. It hardens as it dries.

UK the United Kingdom (England, Northern Ireland, Scotland and Wales)

USA the United States of America

Index